James S. Wilhite M.D.
1899 Parkers Mill
Lexington, Ky
May 22, 1974

Requiem

Requiem

W. J. Tancig

South Brunswick • New York • London

Thomas Yoseloff

Thomas Yoseloff, Publisher
Cranbury, New Jersey 08512

Thomas Yoseloff Ltd
18 Charing Cross Road
London W. C. 2, England

6629
Printed in the United States of America

Wars and battles, in historical retrospect, are usually described in terms of grand strategy, local tactics, and the immortality of generals. Common soldiers are kneaded into a faceless dough of conflict and consigned to oblivion.

This is the story of ordinary soldiers — the days, the nights, the miles and the comradeship — and how they culminate in a vast battle. It begins on the excellent tourist road that threads now among the overgrown Confederate positions. It ends on another.

From the old files I have scrounged names of some men who were there — men with rifles in their hands. Go with them and their venerable regiments for awhile, and test their days and determination and despair.

Stand where they stood — Virginia, West Virginia, Maryland, Pennsylvania — Gettysburg, July 1863.

Requiem

How fine this road where then was none,
Look eastward, now, and greet the Yankee sun
Across the Yankee field, breathe Yankee air
Between the shadowed trees, recall despair.
Here — a picnic ground behind the ridge,
Now, spread your tablecloth, and let it bridge
That century since an Army wept,
Bandaged its wounds, stood guard, and kept
Its fears unspoken, then left its dead to rest.
No corpse will speak,
Eternity would weep.
Shoulder your arms, there is no sleep
With Yankees near.

Y — e — s, lemonade is fine,
Another sandwich? Please,

This was their line,
Shoulder to shoulder across the field,
Brave ranks moved forward, then crossed steel;
Men from Virginia and Tennessee,
North Carolinian infantry,
Alabama, Floridian grit,
Mississippi men were hit;

Mmmm, no — no pickles now; later, please.

The bold were left in those distant trees,
And Pickett's Division, with Pender and Heth,
Spread a bloody cloak for a shrouding sheath.

After '61 and '62,
We thought the Yanks were nearly through,
We'd chopped up their armies, outmatched their skill,
Chased them away from every hill,
Beat all the generals whom they could name,
Proved the South was good at the fighting game,
Thought one last fight, and the North would flee,
If we could lick 'em in '63.
We had Longstreet and Jackson, Hill and Pender,
Fightin' Gordon was a sight to remember,
Ewell and Early, Stuart and Hood,
The Rebs are forgotten, but here they stood.
We've trimmed the meadow, repaired the fence,
And paved the road with reverence,
Erected markers, listed names,
Sold souvenirs on this field of flames;
We've raked the sod, and memories, too,
For those great days the centuries strew,
Till, now, we stand in the battle's mud,
And eye the ground once soaked with blood.

Virginia in May is rainbow fair,
The fields are sweet, tall trees declare
That given some rain, a touch of heat,
The fruit they bear will be honey-sweet.
The grass turned green, Spring showed its charms,
And battle's harvest filled our arms.
From Fredericksburg to the western hills,
Our crop that May was Chancellorsville.

Jackson's Corps scared the blue-coats green,
When out of the trees, like Halloween,
Screamed Rodes and Colston, Heth and Hill,
Flying death's wild shroud for the Yankee kill;
We whipped those Yankees and run them good,
Set fire to their camps like firewood,
Ate up their suppers and stole their guns,
Turned their generals to simpletons;
If Day had rested instead of raced,
We'd put the hare in his proper place,
But Night arrived in a Yankee panic,
And saved them a swim in the Rappahannock.
Their flank rolled back to Hooker's tent,
And they stared at the flames our cannon sent,
Till deep in the brush, and under trees,
Dusk sheltered our jubilant companies.

Soaked from running, and etched with grime,
We tried to sleep for the thousandth time,
Alerted hunger, then fed it fear,
But trusted night to the cannoneer.
Fitful sleep and fitful wake,
The night's too long and dawn won't break.
Awake? Of course,
How many soldiers find
Sweet peace among the chills
And hours of night?
More often know the reeling blow,
The shock, inside a boiling field of summer.
Sleep is a fool wrapped up in Life's chagrin,
What can a soldier fear, once hope is sown?
Let Night begin.

11

Death stalked proud as a grenadier,
Courted our drummer's boyish tear,
Jostled the wounded and laughed when pain
Twisted the trees like a hurricane;
Challenged the pickets and tested posts,
Then passed his dead like martial ghosts.

Now night has fled, mark well the sound,
For Paxton's dead, and Jackson's down.
But still we'll fight, and Yanks will flee
When faced with the might of Bobby Lee.
Marshall the cannon, assault the hill,
Press the fight till their guns fall still,
Push to the river and watch them cross,
We've won the battle, but yet we've lost.
For out of the brush and along the track,
In marching order we're pulling back,
Back to the meadows and out of the damp,
On fields and hills we're making camp.
Rags to be mended, horses shod,
Skin to be hemstitched, praise to God,
Letters need writing, loved ones would hear
If Heaven's heart chased Death to the rear.
Replenish each cartridge, cap and ball,
Guns are for tumblin' the Yankee wall.
Argue for rations, give us some meat,
Slosh is for greasing the Yankee retreat.
Answer formations, ask for a leave,
The cap'n's not giving a Yankee reprieve.

Word's goin' around that Jackson is dead.

Bull Run River in '61,
Stonewall Jackson's just begun,
Harper's Ferry, Front Royal, too,
Staunton to Luray, out of the blue.
Onward to Richmond, fate has no fear,
Though Jackson, its hero, is slow to appear.
Northward to Brandy, march into fame,
Stonewall has flanked 'em, and Bull Run's the game.
Sharpsburg's September, consummate skill,
Lee, Jackson and Longstreet martialed our will.
Fighting for Christmas, Fredericksburg's height,
Yanks dead for nothing, Burnside's last fight.

Form up the men, sergeant —
Yes, suh, cap'n.
Hurry up, theah, fall in, fall in.
Youah at attention, mistuh.
You, Jed, there, and Jubal, too,
Quit yo' cussin' o' Yankee blue,
Dress youah ranks like ol' Jack sed,
And time will show you the Yankee dead.

13

Attention to General Orders —
Headquarters, Army of Northern Virginia,
Effective immediately this army is reconstituted,
And will now consist of three Army Corps.
First Corps, General James Longstreet commanding,
Will consist of General Hood's division, General McLaw's division,
And General Pickett's division — God have mercy on them.
Second Corps, General James Ewell commanding,
Will consist of General Early's division,
General Johnson's division — there goes the Stonewall brigade,
And General Rode's division.
Third Corps, General A. P. Hill commanding,
Ol' Hill and Jackson shore could strike sparks off each other,
But, man, how he kin march. Why, I recall
The purty sight he made just last Fall
Up on Antietam Creek — I still see
Him and his red shirt ridin' up the road
From Ha'per's Ferry — leadin' his division right into line,
To win the battle with that double-time —
Will consist of General Anderson's division,
General Heth's division, and General Pender's division.

With General Jackson's untimely death
I ask each of you for your prayer and for
Even greater effort
In our Just cause.

R. E. Lee, General, Commanding.

Serg — e — a — n — t! Dismiss the company.
Compan — e — e, dismiss'd.

The dead lie dead, their morrows all the same,
Graves win no fights, nor victories attain.
Thus, this end of May, farewell to Spring,
What might have been let no one sing.

Cook up the rations, rags to the rear,
Strip to a soldier's fightin' gear,
Patch up the shoes, boys, find me a hat,
This rebel army is growin' fat.
Load up the caissons and strike our tents,
Stand shoulder to shoulder with Providence.
Company-columned, time's on our hand,
Form for the marching, now wait for command.
Wild rumors are running, sideways and back,
We're headed for Frederick or Frontenac,
Keep an ear to the ground, and one in the wind,
For news will sing like a javelin.

Stuart's gone, with all brigades,
Left a screen, far out, like a balustrade,
Rode to the north with Hampton and Jones,
Robertson, Lees, and the band o' bones,
Sabers and bridles and oats and corn,
Feathers to dance with a saddle horn.

McLaw's men left on the third of June,
With Rodes that night like a witch's broom,
Early and Johnson, of Ewell's Corps,
Off on the fifth toward the Valley's door,
And the shady trees in that sweet June sun,
Fell behind as our march begun.

As long as he's moving a soldier's fine,
But give him food for an anodyne,
A handful of corn, a slab of bacon,
Hot cup of brew for the stomach's quakin',
There's seldom enough from dawn till dusk,
But what there is soothes the body's husk.
Take to the road with an ol' gum sheet,
And taste the stones on calloused feet,
Walk till your rifle's grown to your hand,
Rest in the stubble, beard of the land,
Measure the miles while the dust and dirt
Dye your hair like a butter-nut shirt;
Sweat like a race-horse, bother the smell,
Soldier's bouquet bounds the highway to Hell.
Weary in the mornin', haggard at noon,
Labor till evening spins its cocoon,
Blanket in the shadows, freeze in the damp,
Too cold for movin', sleep with a cramp,
Trust to the sentries, pickets and God,
Rest for tomorrow's promenade.

In spite of the rush to get to war,
There's always one general who feels a chore
To line up his troops that all may see
The men whom he leads to their destiny.
Clean up the patches and practise a cheer,
Send all our misfits far to the rear,
Dress up the columns and get them in line,
Then let them wait on the general's sweet time.

My Dear General Hood, said the invitation,
On the seventh of June, at Brandy Station,
Will be reviewed by R. E. Lee,
Our magnificent southern cavalry;
Bring your people and be my guest,
Your rank will add to the martial zest.
Respectfully, J. E. B. Stuart, Genl.

On the eighth of June, the tale is told,
Hood gathered his people into the fold,
Promised them all a Southern treat,
Then marched forthwith to the Brandy meet.

Latter that day, in the afternoon,
A rumbling sound stirred Stuart's plume,
Caused him to send an aide to see
Who trespassed against his cavalry.

Out of the dust that filled the air,
Galloped the aide in great despair,
Well, lieutenant, is it bad or good?
General, sir, it's General Hood,
Come with his people, the Texas throng;
And General, sir, ten thousand strong!

Well, you tell Hood, now listen, son,
I expect his troops to share our fun,
But I'll skin the man who plays a fool,
Shouts, "Jin'ral Stuart, here's your mule!"

I guess Lee was happy with what he found,
Though he rode so hard he wore them down;
The colors were bright, and the sight was grand,
And war seemed far from our promised land.

It was lucky they rested on the eighth,
Putting things back the way they were,
And taking the shine off.
That was one time, though, the ninth, I mean,
When Stuart refused to believe his own men.
Over Kelly's and Beverly Ford
Raced Pleasanton's U.S. Cavalry horde,
Struck west and north, fought hard and tough,
And Stuart's best waren't good enough.
Lomax and the 'leventh Virginia rode off,
And Cobb's Legion,
And soon it was "Lige" White's battalion,
And Florman's Sixth Virginia.
Then all at once there went
The Jeff Davis Legion, with
The First North Carolina, the
First South Carolina, and Asher Harman's
Twelfth Virginia with Hart's Artillery,
And Lord knows how many others.
But in the end ol' Jeb asked Rodes
To send his men — those columns strode
With speed, and when the night turned fine,
We finally held the river line.

Bury your men, Jeb, muffle the drum,
For all you know there's worse to come.

At last the tenth of June — forget the show,
Desert these camps and test war's vertigo,
Form again for the marching, soldier's chore,
Dance with the dust of walking, evermore.
Let us speed the miles for their taking,
Cuss each joint for its aching,
Savor the bite of each belt and strap,
Grunt at our sweaty habitat,
Jeer at the wagon missing a wheel,
Envy the teamster caught in the deal,
Wonder who's really the principal fool,
You, the teamster, the wagon, or mule.
Wait for each pause by the side of the road,
Pillow your pains with the ant and the toad,

Drink all your water well before noon,
Share your great thirst with every dragoon;
Jaw for the rations, still to be born,
Savor some pigskin, a handful of corn;
Moving, keep moving, push forward, press on,
Through the fields and the mountains, the valleys beyond.
Turn at each hill crest, in wonder behold
The miles of this army, a devil's patrol,
Here is the South that all should see,
Butternut choir and symphony,
Conceived in cotton and born to find
The cannon's fruit is color-blind;
Called from the prairie and pounding shore,
Snatched from each hamlet by sagamore,
Ride from the valleys, lonely glade,
Laugh in the sunshine, die in the shade,
Writ their names for all to see,
Then marched smart for Eternity.
They grumbled and cussed like a weaning pup,
But their courage stayed when the Yanks come up.

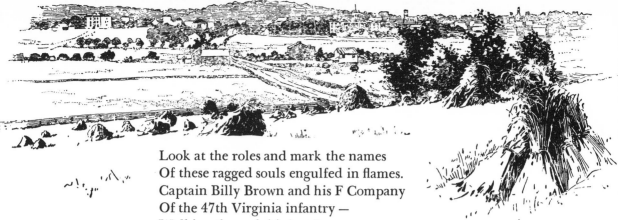

Look at the roles and mark the names
Of these ragged souls engulfed in flames.
Captain Billy Brown and his F Company
Of the 47th Virginia infantry —
Walking through his last June.
And Bartlett Yancy Malone,
Irishman and cornerstone —
H Company, 6th North Carolina.
Private Jesse Jobson, Mississippi son,
Nearly finished, years barely begun.
Thomas Cooper, 'Kuppa' we say,
Daniel Howard and Ephraim Gray,
Jones and Tatum, Baker and Lown,
Anchor and Olson, Sedgwick, Brown,
Skeeter and Mosely, Judson, Grew,
Andrew Hansen, and 'lijah Shrew,
Sergeant Finney and Corporal Pace,
'Beauty' Wheeler and 'Ol Hoss' Race,
Taliaferro, White and Manacone,
Stachon, Hunt, and Reuben Stone,
Schumacher, Shumate, Casher, Ward,
'Hunter' White and Darrell Cord.
Long is the line in this marching game,
But the South has need of every name.

There is no strolling when an army moves,
Although some generals are quick to say
That certain units are usually slow,
Spending more time stopped than on the go.
But get there, all units must,
And if it takes three generals,
Saddled, spurred, and staffed,
There'll be three generals
To talk to the colonels,
Threaten the majors,
Counsel the captains,
And ignore the lieutenants.
Whatever it takes, the troops will move.

Sometimes, if you can remember,
It needs a T. J. Jackson
To ride beside the line of march,
Stuck in the saddle and short of sleep,
Gruff and crowing, his voice would creep
Full of need up every spine,
And yo'd try again to speed the line.
"Close up, close up," was Jackson's plea,
Considered his men foot-cavalry.

Start with the head of the column, then,
A little faster men,
Press on, we can't be late.
Then work down the line of troops,
Close up, men, close up — you're slowing down,
But at the rear he'd turn around
And do the whole thing in reverse;
String us out from the head,
Tread on the heels from the tail,
Somehow the army had to hurry
Before its time ran out.

General Ewell seemed hard to start
At any dawn,
But on the road his staff would chant
Their single tune — Press on, press on.
A. P. Hill of Sharpsburg fame,
Didn't think marching much of a game,
But an army's way to move,
As work to be done,
And he eased it some.
Start a little early, get the men underway,
Yield a little slack in the heat of the day.
No matter how — the army got there,
Or it got new generals.

From twenty miles out, it's there to see,
The Blue Ridge dressed in its panoply,
Smoke on the horizon,
And a whisper in the road,
The grade is slowly rising,
Feel your load, feel your load.
The men who've been there before
Shift their packs a little higher,
Dig their chins into their chests;
By noon the smoke is a blue-gray
Cloud grown to the horizon,
And by three o'clock the officers

Are looking for fields for a night camp.
Again, by dawn we strain
To separate the sky and cloud,
Though, when the line is clean,
We're half an hour along
Our struggle to the pass.
Pass? They may call it that
In man's strange way, by then
Our hearts are pounding fast
As we would like to run
Going down, down, down the other side.

Who can spell the Valley's beauty
Silvered in the distance haze,
Magic of the Shenandoah —
Oktibbeha County never looked like this,
Not even when morning mist rises up
To ghost away from Noxubee Creek,
Nor Calhoun County, or Crawford,
Kershaw, Caswell or Princess Anne.

What did that officer say?
Press on, press on — no, that I heard,
Something about Ewell at Winchester —
Oh, chasing Milroy — great, mighty great,
Sounds like Stonewall's guiding fate,
Except this time, along the Valley Pike,
The whole blamed army will drive the final spike.

June fourteenth — straight north our line,
Berryville, Charles Town, Shepherdstown and Martinsburg,
Rest for the night — sleep on your arms,
We're nearly in Yankee land,
And Yankees fight.
Nearby is Berkeley Springs,
My paw's from there,
Why he went to Texas, I declare
I know now, if all those farms
Are rocky as these fields about;
This shale and layered slate
Ain't much for crops — for goats it's great,
But wait, let night restore
As it has done a million nights before.

Look at the campfires in the hills,
Not fer cookin', but chasin' chills,
Until you turn away —
Gawd-a-mighty, the night is wringin' damp,
Jed — Potomac's t'other side o' camp.
Rode's across, today, I heard, by Williamsport,
Tomorrow we use the ford — a bath of sort.
Look at the mist, like cotton being flung,
Fire? Where? The east?
Why, Jed, the moon is hung.

The army slows at a river crossing,
Catches its breath and goes to pausing,
Double-hitches the cannon, checks each wagon,
Fills each canteen like a golden flagon,
Water the horses, test belt and knot,
Our food ain't much, but it's all we've got.
Form your men for the river's dance,
An', last of all, remove yo' pants.
Keep to the ford, men, water's waist high,
Moving, keep moving, keep the guns dry,
Faster, lieutenant, double your ranks,
You in the gum sheet, hurry your shanks.

Major D-e-n-n-i-s-o-n-n-n-n !

C-o-m-i-n-g, colonel.

Major, are those carriages I see on the other side?
Yes, sir, four of them, colonel, waiting to cross.
Why wait? The ford is wide, signal them to move
But sir, they're young ladies, sir — can't advance,
Remember, sir, the troops have doffed their pants.

Well, major, they have my sympathy, I'm sure,
But this is war; motion them on, let them mature.

Good — good, major, forget the men — they'll have their say,
Let our precious fillies turn away
Lest modesty should make them blind.
Here they come, major, our best apology
For smudging such maidenly purity.

Good morning, madam, so sorry, sorry —
Yes, madam, the army of Northern Virginia.
Yes, madam, the whole army.
Crossing the ford? Yes, madam.
General Lee? Coming along, madam.

Colonel, weren't our virgins rather gay?
Yes, major, and did you notice?
No one turned away!
Some tale they'll tell, what looks they'll draw,
But, still, how many women ever saw
Ten thousand men in one fell swoop,
Dressed in a jay-bird birthday suit.

Let us cross over the river, major.

The north bank is Maryland,
Land of southern comforts and influence,
But eyeing northern affluence;
Armed its men for both the sides,
How can it help but win —
Forget the men who die.
Above the river flats is Williamsport,
And three more easy hours to Hagerstown.
Straight through the streets our martial tread
Drummed out a silence, strangers fled,
But count the cakes and cheers galore,
The smiles and handshakes by the score,
A tear or two, young girls to wave,
Quick preening by our bearded braves.

The best of the shouts and clapping hands
Went for our 1st Marylands,
They'd spruced up themselves, beat off the dust,
Shouldered their arms with a telling thrust,
Tightened their packs and steadied their gait,
Then straightened their ranks to demonstrate,
That though they could fight, they could also stride
To the beat of the heart of Southern pride.

North of Hagerstown we rested for a few days,
And tried to convince our bodies they were refreshed
Partly we were waiting for the artillery
To catch up with us and rest their teams;
Partly we had walked our shoes to pieces,
And needed replacements,
And partly we just got too far ahead of the Army.
Stuart, and the rest of us, seemed
To have lost the Feds.
Somewhere they were east of the mountains —
Behind us, probably, certainly not ahead —
Not the way they ambled along.

June twenty-second, eighteen sixty-three —
We struck our tents at dawn,
Bolted our breakfast and filled
The Chambersburg pike before sun-up.
For awhile I thought old Jack was back,
With Ewell taking up the slack.
Close up, close up, we've miles to go,
And Pennsylvanians by the score to show
This army's in the field to fight.
And one thing more — stay in the ranks —
Enemy country — no Rebel pranks,
Details will gather stock and horses in.
These people will not like our actions, true,
But we shall do what must be done,
March, and strike, and overrun.
Our target, if you want to know,
Is Harrisburg — with sixty miles to go.

When you march with Ewell you lead the van,
Scout the road and explore the land,
Stir up the farmers, crowd each town,
Start the day's walking 'fore breakfast's down.
March for fifty, then rest for ten,
Shoulder your pack and do it again.

An Army on the move is a weary sight,
Fifteen miles of wagons, guns and dirty men
Along the roads, starting and stopping,
Stretching an ear, when officers gather
In conference near. Trotting to prod
Some laggards on, or sitting
To watch their marathon.

A tight little band of men?
Not this army, nor this Corps.
When Ewell's men get underway,
He has fifty-six infantry regiments
On the move, plus three separate battalions,
Plus the artillery, plus the wagons.
Mouth these numbers and watch his men,
Though the years have fled they counted then —
Five Alabama regiments — 3rd, 5th and 6th,
The wondrous 12th and 26th.
Ten more regiments from Georgia;

The 4th, the 12th, 13th and 21st,
The 26th, 31st, 38th, 44th, 60th and 61st.
Ten regiments from Louseeann,
Hell-bent to fight, the 1st, the 2nd,
5th, 6th, 7th, 8th and 9th,
The 10th, the 14th and 15th.
Maryland? The staunch 1st Maryland battalion.
Terrapin state? Her men moved
Like they were out to speed up fate.

Sixteen long regiments from North Carolina,
Stoutly blessed by their 1st and 2d North Carolina battalions.
The 1st, 2d, 3rd, 4th, 5th and 6th,
The 12th, 14th, 20th, 21st and 23rd,
The 32nd, 43rd, 45th, 53rd and the 57th.
And from Virginia, the Old Dominion,
They counted fifteen regiments for the line,
The 2d, 4th, 5th, 10th and 21st,
Their 23rd, 25th, 27th, 31st and 37th,
The 42nd, 48th, 49th, 50th and the 52nd.

And still, numbers cannot march or fight,
Have you tasted the names of those whose might
Has steeled the ranks with ball and flame?
Forget the generals, they've had their day,
Count each lone man in our ranks of gray.
Start with 16 year old Willie Mitchell from Virginia . . .
W — i — l — l — i — e, where are yo' now, Willie?
Or private Wesley Culp, soon to die
On Culp's Hill — named for his gran'pap.
Caldwell, Lewis — Owen and Wood,
Johnston, Irby, Morgan and Good,
Chamberlaine, Daniel, Dickert and Hahn,
Merrick, Dick Fletcher, and Jason Johns,
Childers, Barbee, Dooley and Giles,
Dunaway, Thompson, and Jeffrey Miles,
Poague and Willis, Blackburn and Flynn,
March till you're weary, then fight to win.

Greencastle, Chambersburg, Carlisle,
And then Harrisburg, across the river.
But once we passed the Pennsylvania line,
The natives' looks near turned to brine,
And how they wept
To see their horses, hogs,
Their cattle, fowl and grain,
Seized by our men and driven off.
Somehow they seemed to think that Milroy
Could plunder through the Valley — that was WAR!
But take *their* stock? We're but a bandit horde;
And proof? We're living by the sword.
What futile screams and tears,
How often did they plead their waning years,
And yet, when those lusty draft horses were led
Beside each caisson's tongue
And harnessed up,
It did us good to watch the silken power
And well-fed frames step out to war
Beyond the farming lanes.

The fields were green, but not yet ripe,
Still, since we had their stock, we'd best
Take grain and fill our empty wagons.
Oats and corn, oats and corn and hay,
An army lives on the fruit of the fields,
Black or crimson, green or gold,
Beef or barley, cooked or cold,
Trample the stubble, bother the yields,
Load the wagons with oats and hay,
Or this Army will die from day to day.

Blessings from the 23rd of June.
I lie abed this dawn
Beneath my bush and bough —
The day'll be fine, and yet, somehow
There's something changed — a quiet
Seldom heard before. Our sentry whistles
At a morning bird whose head is cocked
As if he's heard this interlude — soliloquy.
Unwind my bandaged blanket, feel
Day's chill touch — catch the sentry,
"Why the quiet? What has changed?"
"Quiet? Oh, Stuart's gone to hound
The Yanks. That's all, not much."
Not much! No wonder Day's asleep —
No messenger each hour or so,
To pound the gravel
Throwing news or jibes to us who walk.
But if Stuart and his clan have fled,
Who's left to screen us from the Yanks ahead?
To check road crossings, each country town,
Scout valleys while we hold the heights,
Then lead us down.

Not Grumble Jones and his hill-bred flock,
Slow to fight but they love to talk,
Mounted on nags for all to see
The least of our saddle-sore cavalry.
Left to themselves, they fuss and scold,
Give them Stuart, they're big and bold,
Most of the time they're rough as a cob,
You send for their help, and they're late for the job.

Give me a teamster instead.

And that leaves Beverly Robertson —
Not much,
Aims to please, lacks a leader's touch.
Find him a mission, instinctively
He'll gallop to hell, reliably.
Around our camps he'll pound and sweep,
His men'll be worn, but the Yanks will sleep,
The mounts will fail and his men will fade,
If they're part of Robertson's horse parade.

The word's coming along now . . .

Mount up some of your teamsters and
Get them out towards Quincy and Cashtown,
Roxbury, Dickinson, Hunters Run,
Don't let the Yankees spoil our fun,
Close up the columns, take up the slack,
This Army's not ready for turning back.

June twenty-sixth for Jubal Early
Was to leave Ewell go his way toward Carlisle,
Then plod along the Cashtown road.
Burn the iron works at Greenford, but push on.
Touch the morning mist tangled in the hills,
Climb the hanging trail to Cashtown,
The crests held no relief for old Jube, rest your horse, General,
Nor any fear —
Gordon in the van,
Hoke next,
Then Extra Billy Smith,
And Hay's brigade to shield the rear.

37

Push on, push on, once through the dwindling hills speed up the gait,
The country's flat, don't make the Yankees wait.

Straight down the pike to ride the tail of June,
Church spires in sight,
Another town to shock at noon,
With guns and men, wagons and rags,
And a steady banter from curbstone wags.
"What dirty looking men," some woman said,
"Why, ma'am," called Sergeant Drew,
"We always wear old clothes for a hawg killin'."
Not nice, but true.

The railway station sleeps beside the square,
The cobbles in the street are hot to touch,
Most townsmen stay inside
But look out through a slanted door,
Or stand behind their lilac hedge.

We'd hardly come into the town before
We left it's easter side to shuffle
Through more country dust.
"Say, Cap'n," someone in H Company
Of the 13th Georgia asked,
"What town was that?"
"It sho' warn't Panola."
"Rest easy, son, and cool your urge,
"That shabby place is Gettysburg."
"Well, whoever heard of Gettysburg?"
But there we stayed, though orders kept us close to camp,
Rest in the roadside pastures, savor the evening's damp.

The next morning we collected ourselves,
And some more of the local cattle and grain,
Working east again. This way we'll soon
Surround 'most all the Yankee states,
And while they search for Lee
We'll win the war and Jube
Will slump in his saddle and listen
While Billy Smith tells all these Yankees
How wrong they are, and how we 'uns only want to go home;
"Well, what's keeping you?" someone asks.
"We rather like our outing here — perhaps we'll stay awhile."

"Gin'ral Smith," Jubal shouts from half a block away,
"Ah think you'd best move on, suh,
"An' save yo' speechin' fo' anuthuh day."

Our east-bound road went straight to York,
And what a shock those townsmen took
When Early said he wanted eight and twenty thousand dollars,
Forty thousand pounds of beef, thirty thousand bushels of corn,
And a thousand pairs of shoes.
They scurried 'round, and pounded doors,
Met here and there,
But finally brought the money,
And all the other things.

Early had it packed away that 28th of June,
And in our camp outside of town,
Sunday, as it turned out to be,
We had some quiet church services
While details worked the farms
And found more heavy cattle, grain galore,
Stout teams to pull the guns,
And wagons by the score.
More barrels of flour, farm harness,
Tubs of sauerkraut —

Gordon's brigade, foot-cavalry beyond a doubt,
Faster than "Lige" White's cavalry Rangers,
Pushed toward Columbia, beyond
The Susquehanna river, to burn the bridge,
But Dutch militia set it to fire, and Gordon's men
Worked to keep Wrightsville from burning to the ground.
Little to report: no Yankee army here,
No troops abroad, the farmers' tears are melons
As they watch their barns give forth — somehow
They think they are beyond the war
And immune. So, let them plough
Their fantasies and plant Jeff Davis dollars,
Harvest these ranks of rebel grey,
Butternut hearts and aching feet,
Drink up the vintage of '63,
And savor the taste of war's defeat.

Monday, June 29th, eighteen sixty-three,
Form the brigades, prepare to march, now let us see
If we can capture Harrisburg, state capitol and such,
Strike up the bands, march through the streets,
Let Ewell scare the Dutch.

An easy day's march from York,
Though we must herd the stock along,
And cart the Yankee truck,
I wonder what the cows will do
When Early says, "Close up!"
Another hour or so before we leave,
Gather in lazing groups to grieve
That we must march in threatening rain,
Sample the mud in each country lane,
Sweat in a gum sheet, soak if you've none,
Cuss with your column in unison.
Check on your rations, bacon and corn,
Our hunger's hope is a love forelorn.

What's that, sergeant? The march is stayed?
Back to the fields for another day?
Sounds like the gin'rals have got out of hand,
What! Lee's found the Yanks in Yankee land!
W'all now, that sounds like fun,
When do we start fer Washington?
Tomorrow, you say? Where? Heidlersburg?
Sounds like another German scourge.
West of York? Well, I hope there's sun
To dry the roads till the race is done.
Twenty some miles is Tuesday's fare,
Good, good. We'll meet the rest of Two Corps there,
Then Ewell, casting his eye for bigger game,
Can seek the heat of the devil's flame.

The rhythm that shuffles a soldier's feet
Snakes through the miles like a tuned deceit,
Collects each hour as a chord to hum,
But rolls each step like a kettle-drum.
Begins each day with a sprightly gait,

Then shakes its cares like a celibate,
Shorten the road in the morning,
Make it forever at night,
Bother the soldier who stumbles,
Sing of the comfort in sight.
Tell of the cool in the evening,
Rivers that sweetly caress,
Delude with the dust and the distance,
Charm with a love's tenderness.
Shuffle-step-shuffle-step-shuffle,
Look to the turn in the road,
Wait for the ten in each sixty,
Live by the shuffle-step-shuffle-step code.

Another day of marching, hurry on,
Another day of sweating marathon,
Uncoil these miles of gravel,
Spin out their endless ravel,
And in the soldier's fashion,
Cuss out each moment's passion,
The hunger, thirst, the captain,
But hurry on.

All roads still lead to nowhere, change their names,
Strike out the rutted cart tracks, stones disclaim,
Forget their ragged winding,
Their burning and their blinding,
And in our hurry, squander
Day dreams tossed out to wander
With the hunger, thirst and captain,
Hurry on.

Two miles east of Heidlersburg
Early's seventeen regiments made camp for Tuesday night,
Their last night of June.
The last June had some but known it.
An easy day's march, even in the bare feet
That many wore.
Make the fires and roast the meat,
Roast, rest and groan,
But eat, eat, eat
This farming food that Early found.
Tomorrow we may go to ground,
And dig out Yankees hiding there.
Heat up the biscuits, fry the beans,
Drink up those boiled out roastin' greens,
Sate weariness with hunger, test hope's wan score,
We've one day less to fight the war.

There is no doubt in the marching mind
When fighting's in the air,
The countryside may slumber,
The day be bright and fair,
No cannon's snort will lumber,
Take up this army's dare,
But men will set to talkin', hopes appeal,
"Say, Dan, no matter what you say, I got the feel,
"There's shootin' up ahead, a job fer steel."
"I feel the same," he says, "And so do I,"
And purty soon the columns notify
Their captains that the warning's said,
And men will check each cartridge, heft their lead,
Shift packs, pull down each hat, and grip each sling,
The column tightens up and miles take wing.

Gordon, Hays, Hoke and Smith,
Early's seven thousand demons lost no time
Filling the Harrisburg road that morning.
Heidlersburg to Gettysburg, the circuit's nearly done,
The march is slow, and yet, by ten declare
This is the day for Yanks, and fightin's in the air.
By half past noon we heard the guns' soft yawn,
And Jubal spurred beside — "Push on, push on,
"P — u — s — h   o — n."

If you marched with Gordon's brigade
That first of a new July,
You came from Georgia —
Six regiments raised between the Floridian sea,
The fields of Carolina and the mountains of the Cherokees.
You fought well
Because your general fought well;
He fed his men, demanded discipline, kept up his records,
And never left his wounded behind.
When he put you to battle he expected to win,
And so did each of those six regiments —
If you couldn't do it, it couldn't be done,
But he tipped his hat when the ground was won.

Two o'clock in the scorching bright
Of that Yankee sun, and the road led straight
Toward the cannon's snarl —
Skirmishers lined out and the march slowed down
As we spied the spires of Gettysburg town,
The guns come up and the words retreat
And our hearts thump out in the summer's heat.
West of us, fightin' on the right,
Rebs were moving in, making quite a sight —
"That's Rodes out there," our rumors claimed,
And if it was they fought like they were lame,
Though it was kinda hard ter see,
Their music was no ordered symphony,
The trumpets and the drums seemed all mixed in,
With fiddles, flags and fortune chorusing out a hymn.

A clatter of horses, and shouts to spare,
"Off the road, by the flank — form over there!"
"Thirteenth G-e-o-r-g-i-a-a-a, follow m-e-e-e-e."

And then there were calls for the twenty-sixth Georgia,
The thirty-first, thirty-eighth,
The sixteenth — those Bartow Invincibles,
And the sixty-first from DeKalb and Montgomery.
And Gordon followed out beside the line,
To check its dress,
And then to press
Us forward for the fight.
"Keep to a walk, don't start to run,
"Press onward now, 'fore Rodes comes all undone."
Rodes! Let Rodes ride off to hell,
There's blue-coat cavalry ahead, they'll not compel
This line to wait.

47

"Hey, Ben," young Yoder nods to me,
"Look yonder," and to our left, across the road
Are Hays' men forming up,
Forming and moving forward,
There's Early hunched horse-high,
Spittin' tobacco while he keeps his eye
On these brigades that Jackson trained to war,
Lord, the miles we marched for that man.

Listen to those carbines pop, too far away
To hurt us, let them go,
Weak screen of horsemen — there, watch them flee,
Heads up now, men, we've Yankee infantry
Beyond this corn and wheat.
And through the trees,
What miserly creek is this? Tramp down the brush
Along its banks, plunge in its muddy wet,
And let your sodden boots match up
Each shirt that's soaked with Wednesday's sweat.
Up the bank and check your bayonets,
Close up those ranks, let's have a yell,
F-o-r-w-a-r-d a-n-d F-I-R-E,
Reload, and hold the line,
Move on again — those Yanks are swine,
Look at their flags — they're Dutchmen on that hill,
The ones we broke — who ran at Chancellorsville.

Ben Yoder trips and goes down on his face,
But when I try to grab his hand
The bloody bubbles weave their lace
Beside his chest —
Oh, Ben — by damn —
Back to the line and feed the lead
Across the sweltering field,
Faster, still faster, our line has come
Till now we're moving near a run,
No time to load, let them taste steel
Till every bloody Dutchman
Knows how young Ben Yoder feels.
They've broke agin — there, watch them run,
Back to the town and oblivion.

Slow your ranks, men,
Gawd, I'm out of wind
And gasping like a sway-back horse.
Keep the line moving and close up the ranks,
Yes, suh, cap'n, ah'll sho' try,
But you breathe for me, cap'n,
Just tell me why
Ben Yoder was the only man this company lost.

We're comin' into town, and — why, look
At all the bluecoats standin' round —
Gave up the fight.
An' here comes Gordon, a pretty sight
Across the field, cheered to win the race,
If you can call it that.
Put your damned hat back on, general,
You've had your cheer,
Now tell Ben Yoder's maw
What happened here.

Yes, suh, lieutenant, ah sho' will halt and rest,
Here, share my shade, suh, that sun is quite a pest.

Most of the times we fought and chased
Running Yanks all over the place,
We had to stop when night came down,
Or roads were jammed with the tumble-down
Of fleeing troops, too tired to win,
But scared to lose under discipline.
This afternoon, when we were into them,
And through them,
The word was passed to break it off —
Just let them run away.
But why, we asked, they'll only fight another day.
Even Gordon seemed mad with the order,
Dismounted, he snapped, then swung his hat
Against a tree.
Later galloped off to Early, or to Ewell,
But there we stayed,
And south of town, along a gentle ridge,
Let Yankees spend their day.

By dusk we'd ate and cleaned
The powder off our face,
Got out o' town and closed up to the hills,
Though at their bottom was our spot,
Dang fools, we said, let's take the top.
Kick out the fire 'fore bullets start to yell,
Tomorrow'll be a scorcher,
Between the sun and hell.

Goodnight, Ben Yoder,
We'll miss you, boy, and yer maw'll miss you,
And those Georgia fields'll miss you.
You fought real well, Ben. Good luck fer now.

At daybreak on the second they got us up —
Feed yourselves before we fight, the word was sped,
Then, having ate, we moved back to better ground,
And sat and sat and sat while Day just bled.

Sometime after noon we listened to a battle
South of us, and then it seemed to drift our way.
All that afternoon we waited,
But no order got to us.
Well, light up the fires, let's eat 'fore dusk,
Day may be over,
But cookin''s a must.

Sit on the edge of battle, wasted day,
Live for an extra hour or two, far away,
Sun at the zenith lays useless,
Men on the ground rest worn,
Fear is our ration for hunger,
Fry up the bacon and corn.
Dusk is our promise of evening,
Sip our charred brew as at ease,
Here on the lip of a battle,
Night blankets day's sound that would seize.

What fool is blowing that bugle? Assembly?
Why, I've hardly finished eating.
For us, sergeant? I'm not surprised,
Fall in and dress the line,

F-o-r-w-a-r-d, and take that hill ahead,
We'll need cat's eyes if night won't wait,
Howard's Dutchmen sit on top —
Well, we've chased them twice,
Get out the bayonets and scream them to death.
Hoke is coming on our left,
And Rodes is promised for the right,
Though he's so far behind in town
He may not beat the night.
Through the slough and over the fence,
Those rascals still can run —
Up the hill, now, and at the stone wall,
Keep it up, Yanks, your fire is high,
It suits us fine, when we're with Hays
We have no wish to die.
How much higher is that hill?
And where is Rodes?
What? One more line to win,
Now at them, boys, a final thrust
For old Dick Taylor —
Louisiana Tigers on the hunt . . .
There, we're through, now at the gunners,
And Hoke's in sight —
The hill is ours, at least for now,
Thank God for dusk and growing night.
But where is Rodes, especially
Since we helped him yesterday,
Our two brigades can't hold the hill,
Eight regiments to dam their army —

Damn you, Rodes, where are you?

Ah, someone's coming on the right,
Rodes? We'll see, hold your fire
Until we're sure they're friends,
All right, boys, let 'em have it —
Three volleys for those 'friends.'
Now, show them how the Tigers roar,
And look, more 'friends' beyond the left —
Forget the guns, men, down the hill,
We've done our best, no earthly skill
Can slow their growing ranks.
And, Rodes, thanks for your support,
Count our Ben Yoders on this hill,
Tell them where you've been, exhort
Their souls to rise and smite

Those hordes atop the crest,
And in the darkness wrap their shrouds
Around your heart, bid them farewell,
This midyear night they did their best.
We should have won these hills
When they were open yesterday,
But, generals, with their puzzled way,
Preferred we wait till Yanks were on display.

Now, Early, nearly hidden in the dark,
Takes stock how close we came to hold
East Cemetery Hill, to trip the Yankees up,
Had Rodes but come — but let him tell
How, when his strength was wanted,
He let us go to hell.

Get some sleep, men, tomorrow we'll fight again,
The night is half-gone now,
Lie down and rest your bones,
Let souls and heart-aches tramp the dark
And fence the fields with memories
Which will not dress these ranks again;
Share canteens and campfires, winter chills,
Corn that is green in the soldier's mouth,
And the long, tired line of the marching South,
Feet that are bare, and backs near bent,
With Jackson dead, and Stuart spent.

Did you see those draggin' horsemen
Came back with Stuart awhile ago?
Out with Extra Billy Smith, now,
On the road to York.
Walkin' death, both men and horses,
Lot of good they'll do.

Get to sleep, men, get to sleep.

Roll up in a gumsheet, clothes that are damp,
Die in the sleeping soldier's camp,
Share in the hunger, fear, mad scheme,
Huddle to earth in exhaustion's dream.

Watch where that horse steps, captain,
This area's full of sleeping men.
Yes, sir, colonel.

The prescription calls for moonlight and marching men,
Mixed up at one-thirty in a morning of July 3d,
And you wont' know whether these are corpses on foot,
Or sleepy men asleep on their feet.

Take two of Rodes' brigades and let Ewell
Shift them to Johnson for a sneak attack
On Culp's Hill. Take Culp's and watch
Those Yankees run, he said. Perhaps
It can be done — though two days late.
We'll strike at day's first gate,
And let the bluecoats heft our weight.

Sit here with Early's men and hear the fight,
Old Allegheny's all alone while on his right
The rest of Ewell's Corps sleeps and grumbles
That they cannot help.
Five to six and seven, to eight and nine,
At last the guns grow cool, but still the line
Stays where it was at five.
Breakfast was blood and cannon shell,
Glory was being blown to hell.

Fight up the hill and then retreat
To try again with aching feet,
Bother Yankees, they'll run in fear,
Hiding behind each cannoneer.
Except, today, we've won the running crown,
Crawled up the hill and then dashed down.
So, let the din die out, the cost too grim,
Another place, another day — we'll try to win.

Is this to be one more day for sitting?
To watch the others place their guns,
Move in more men, committing
To defense, dig shelter's ditch,
Then, consider what must be our scheme,
Bring up more men, more guns, redeem
Their ignorance with a man-made cluster,
While Early, in the noon's warm shade,
Enjoys their bluster?

Noon! he says. Captain, send me
A fast-walking man, one you know
Will use his head, and not let rank bestow
Raw fear,
If faced by a jangling, shouting cavalier.

I've sent for Sergeant Wing, sir,
Twenty-first North Carolina, no nerves, steel bones,
And he moves like a hound on a new-laid trail,
He sees everything, hears everything,
But won't stop to talk.

Ah, Sergeant, I've a joint of cold mutton
For an old friend of mine who'll fight
In an hour or two —
If you can get it through, my compliments
To General Cadmus Wilcox
Of R. H. Anderson's division, Third Corps,
Near the other end of our position.
Now, sergeant, stay behind our lines,
Behind that ridge — that's Rodes to the right —
And, sergeant —
Sir?
Run your errand, boy, but do not stay to fight.

Stop by when you return and let us know
How goes the day.
Thank you, general, an hour will see me there,
An hour's return, another moment, sir, to speak
To a kinsman in the 9th Alabama.

Hurry, sergeant, it's for today's lunch.

Had you been with Sergeant Wing that July day,
You went straight west on the avenue
To the Hagerstown Road, then turned south
And followed the trail behind Pender's position,
Staying off the crest of Seminary Ridge
As far as possible, but still seeing as much as you could.
Your oil-cloth package hangs in a bag
Over your shoulder, kept in place by one hand,
While the other carries your rifle.

Pender's Division seemed to be both coming and going,
And farther on, though lying in the windless shade,
Were full ranks of men waiting to attack over the ridge.
The 47th Virginia infantry regiment, the 55th, the 46th,
And the 22d battalion — the Brockenbrough brigade.
These were jammed into the 11th Mississippi, the 2d
The 42d and 26th, and the 50th North Carolina,
Davis' brigade someone said — and who is Davis?

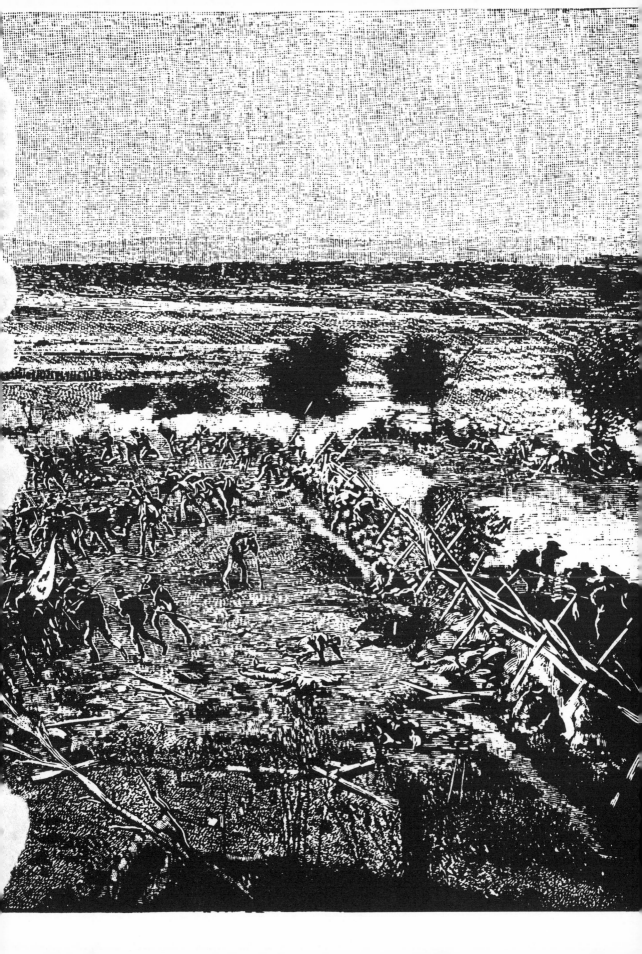

There are some familiar faces, Lane's brigade
From Pender's Division —
This ought to be a mixed up fight,
The 28th North Carolina, the 37th, 7th, 18th, and 33rd,
And more North Carolinians in the Pettigrew brigade,
His 52d, 42d, 11th, 26th and 47th North Carolina regiments.
West country men from Archer's brigade —
Seventh Tennessee, the 1st and 14th Tennessee, the 13th Alabama,
With the 5th Alabama battalion trailin' along.

Another of Pender's brigades at last — this one's Scales',
The 38th North Carolina, the 13th, 34th, 22d, and 16th.
Looks like this is to be mostly a North Carolina attack,
Ah, more Virginians, and Garnett's brigade
With his 56th, 28th, 19th, 18th and 8th Virginia regiments.
Back a little is Armistead's brigade and Virginia's 38th,
Fifty-seventh, 53d, 9th, and 14th infantry regiments.
And, lastly, Kemper's brigade lying in line,
The 3d Virginia, 7th, 1st, 11th and 24th regiments.
Pickett's Division, a man says,
Spent the past year walking,
Chasing and stalking,
But not much fightin',
Give them another hour and they'll
Wish they still were walkin'.

General Wilcox? General Early's compliments, sir,
And his wishes for a pleasant lunch.
Why, sergeant, tell him that both General Garnett and I
Thank him for this culinary treasure,
No doubt, a sample of local farming measure.
I'm sorry we've nothing in return,
But at least today's assault
Will come on a full stomach.
And, sergeant . . .
Yes, sir?
I'd like you to stay here in the shelter
Of this house till the cannonade is over —
Minutes at the most.

But, general, I'll run between the shells,
And General Early wants me back, as well.

Sorry, sergeant, but here you'll stay
So Early can be thanked —
Perhaps to send more food another day.

    *   *   *

Well, General Early, as soon as the cannonade lifted
I headed back, but had to wait
While General Pickett's Division came out of the woods
And started down the ridge.
And then a little farther north the other six brigades
Moved for the field.
Then, while they dressed their line —
Yes, sir, under direct fire —
I moved on, but stopped to watch the attack
From behind General Rodes' division.

The movement seemed at least as daring
As the Federals' fight at Fredericksburg,
And much broader, sir.
Of course, sir, *our* line kept moving toward the hill,
But the brigades at this end of it,
When struck by flank artillery fire —
We had no counter fire, sir —
Seemed to dissolve — the men even ran back.
Very poor, sir, very poor spirit.
The rest kept on, although they were roughly handled
By the Yankee guns — over half down, general,
And though they seemed to get to the crest of the hill —
The Yankee hill, sir,
They were no sooner there than they came tumbling back.
Supporting troops, general?
I saw none, sir, and there was no secondary attack.

It is my impression, sir, the assault was repulsed.
But General Wilcox had your mutton
For lunch, and thanks you mightily for it, sir.
Thank you, sergeant, the job was done
In a style inviting comparison.

When you have assembled your best troops,
Sent them to the attack in God's name,
Seen them near their goal across hard fields
Only to blend with the cannon smoke
And the burning haze of a July afternoon,
Watch but a handful returning
Where you had sent thousands. . . .
No matter the whys and the wherefores,
No matter what man is to blame,
You face the ranks still remaining
And weld them into a frame.
Forget the fear and the heartache,
Be deaf to the cries of defeat,
You, there, stand with your piece to the ready,
And, soldier, up on your feet.
Save your tears for the hearthsides of winter,
Your weariness leave with the dead,

Form into ranks for defending,
And shoot till the terror has fled.

Recall other days when we've wavered,
Other fields where they've battered our weight,
Remember by dark we'd be winning,
And holding the reins of their fate.

Surely there must be some meaning to
The Seven Days' struggle,
Second Bull Run,
The juggernaut of Sharpsburg,
Fredericksburg and Chancellorsville.

Still, day cannot erase night,
Particularly when it is the end of day.

Major, get some food readied for these men,
And hurry —

Yes, sir. At once, sir.

Dusk was a cloak of forgiveness,
Traitorous words dull the glare,
Forget the hours that are passing,
Tomorrow may help us to snare
Those people who've caused this great hurting,
And we shall rush with a scream
Beyond this field of our failing,
And — sleep, soldier, sleep with your dream.

Now, Colonel, I want the ambulances
And wagons to head for Williamsport,
The Potomac crossing, Colonel, via Hagerstown.
No, Colonel, we shall not start tonight.
We are not defeated, colonel, but this campaign
Is now at an end.

General Hill will lead the van,
To be followed by Longstreet —
Send him *written* instructions, Colonel,
And General Ewell will be our rearguard.
I, myself, shall tell Hill and Ewell.

General Stuart will watch the passes
While we return to Virginia.

A sad day, Colonel, but we
Shall soon have other victories.

Get those messages out at once, Colonel,
And remember our columns will not move
Until *I* give the order.

July 4th, 1863, eighty-seven years
Since that first Independence Day,
But both our sides celebrated yesterday.
Today
There sit the Yanks, watching,
Waiting and wondering what we shall do.
Will we attack, stay still, retreat,
Was this a final rendez-vous?

They do not celebrate while burying dead.

Roll the wagons, at last we head for home,
Ten thousand miles to dream, a million hills
For climbing,
And one more crossing of the Potomac,
With the only martial strain
Our wounded in the wagons,
Wrapped with pain.

Let Heaven cry,
Let rain run off our steel,
While ghosting ranks march quickly by,
Sound off Death's roll-call — last appeal.

I want all youah men to form a ring
Here, and hurry up. We've
A long way to go.
First of all, sort youahselves out by States,
Alabama first, and Virginia last, and then
I want the senior sergeant for each state
To arrange you by regiments, and he
Will be responsible for preparing the master roll.

What's that, mistuh? Who am I?
I'm Sergeant-Major Gill, G Company, 18th Virginia,
And General Armistead ordered me
To get this started.

Who asked about rations? Sol'juh,
Where we're going there's no need for rations.

Now youah olduh men look out fer our boys —
This will be a long and hard march,
The last one for all of us,
And the road is steep and rough.
What road you ask? I guess
It's called the Glory Road.

Hustle along, men.

Second Florida Infantry — Jones and Reddick,
Fifth Florida — David Scott, Barnes and Duke,
Bariman, Jones, Oliver, White — faster, men.
We can't spend the night in these chopped up fields.
Calhoun, Cash, Hudson and Cox,
Slaughter and Thomas, Leinten and Rowe —
Sergeant, pass the word when you're set to go.
Dudley Isom, William Osborne, G Company, 11th Mississippi.
And those look like Tennesseans —
McClure and Christon, Allison, Holt,
Stewart and Myrick, Bailiff and Bolt,
Rison and Birdshaw, Holloway, King,
Shackleford, Fizer, Powell and Ring,
McCulloch and Simmons, Wall and Jett. . . .

Let's git along to the North Carolinians,
Marshall and Hedgecock, Erwin and Guy,
Rose and Parker from Company I,
Garrison, Dellinger, Hafner and Smith,
Hayes and Pugh, and Wiley Swift.
Triplett and Curtis, Bryan and Flake,
Fortner and Poovy, Gil Lewis and Lake.
Cheves and Pucket, Utley and Mann,
Sergeant Thompson, move when you can.

And those long ranks must be the Virginians —
Listen how they shout,
Linneous Jones, Tweedy and Stout,
Gilliam, Dowdy, Eckles and Gunn —
Those last two are from my company,
Davis and Spencer, Vermilion and Hix,
St. John and Driscoll have crossed the Styx.

Start your columns, sergeant, colors rolled,
Ranks closed up, this is no stroll,
No cause for straggling, no Yanks ahead,
Lively, step lively, you Southern dead.
No music for luster, no drums to throb,
But we're still an Army, not Satan's mob.
Get those shoulders up, see your backs are straight,
We'll march like men through Heaven's gate.
Cut yo' chattuh, keep those columns true,
F-O-R-W-A-R-D,   m-e-n,
To our last review.

    *   *   *

Look backward as the field grows dim,
March homeward to a dying hymn,
Blend blood and iron and fallen men
As mud, to tell the tale again
To picnics in this lonely wood,
Where Rebs are forgotten,
But here we stood.